Crying for Kharkiv

Six Weeks of Non-War

About the Author

Jim McDonald worked as a professional biologist with an ongoing interest in ecological and environmental issues. He is a published author who uses a reflective and poetic style to convey thoughts on current issues of concern. He writes to challenge and to promote critical reflection on what we consider to be normal and acceptable. He strives for our emotions to dance on the body of the factual, enhancing our reality. In this, he brings a welcome urgency to our adoption of sense in addressing the things that really matter.

Jim McDonald

Crying for Kharkiv

Six Weeks of Non-War

Vanguard Press

A CIP catalogue record for this title is
available from the British Library.

ISBN 978-1-83794-044-8

*Vanguard Press is an imprint of
Pegasus Elliot Mackenzie Publishers Ltd.*
www.pegasuspublishers.com

First Published in 2024

**Vanguard Press
Sheraton House Castle Park
Cambridge England**

Printed & Bound in Great Britain

To the people of Ukraine, in their time of need.

100% of royalties from this book will be donated directly to Hope and Homes for Children, an international charity working in Ukraine since 1998 to ensure each child can enjoy the safety and belonging of a loving family home, never an orphanage. To learn more about their response during the invasion of Ukraine, please visit
www.hopeandhomes.org/ukraine-report

A big thanks to all who read and commented upon the draft version of this work. Those who made critical comment include Yvonne, Karen, Pola and Rick. An especial thanks to Jim and Betty for their shared experience of what poetry means and can do. And, of course, a big thanks to Catriona, who cannot escape my disquiet.

Foreword

Here you will find forty-two poems or, perhaps more informatively, twenty-one pairs of poems. They relate to the first forty-two days of the most recent invasion of Ukraine by Russian soldiers – six weeks of what Putin has referred to as a 'special operation' that is not a war. You will no doubt have made up your own mind on the veracity of that statement. Forty-two poems over forty-two days but not necessarily a poem every day. Sometimes there were two or more poems on the one day. Inevitably there were blank days. I say 'inevitably' because, at times, I found the ability to write was quashed by the utter enormity of events. Unlike many of the people of Ukraine, I could take a break and resume writing when I was refreshed. For many in Ukraine, the notion of a 'break' must be a distant memory.

I cannot, of course, identify with the true horror, distress and grief of the Ukrainian people. To do that, I would have to be one of them. I would have to be on the front line of Putin's wrath and idealism; perhaps a front-line soldier, or maybe just a civilian minding my own business when suddenly it was my turn to be hit. But, in this day and age of instant media coverage, I am bombarded (if I so wish) by the awful truth as it unfolds. And, for better or for worse, I tend to face the bombardment. I say 'truth' because I trust in the accuracy of what I hear from the mouths of the reporters and broadcasters to whom I listen. All of the scenaria – twenty-one poems relating to events in Ukraine – about which I write, are based on the communications of reporters from the BBC and Channel 4 News. In my experience, these broadcasting companies are as good (unbiased) as we are likely to get. I think they largely contribute, with positive and negative critique without undue bias, sometimes to their own detriment. That is surely the stamp of a good and honest broadcaster. There are, of course, many other media outlets of similar integrity. If I do not listen to them, it is because time does not permit that I should listen to them all. Unfortunately, there are others that are much less scrupulous when it comes to matters of 'truth'. We all make choices in these matters and, over the years, I have made mine (and you will have made yours). I have not named reporters (the exception being Orla Guerin of the BBC in the absurdity of 'The Wedding Guest'). They are many, and I have the greatest admiration for them all. They come across as being very brave and compassionate. The twenty-one poems on Ukraine are based entirely on what they reported. I thank them all for their unstinting efforts at keeping us all informed.

Each of the twenty-one scenario poems is preceded by an 'introductory' poem, something that loosely paves the way for the main sentiment that is to follow. Sometimes this introductory statement is quite specific and has been written in the context of the 'event'. In the category of such specifics are 'Saturation Point', 'Composure', 'Convenience of Conscience', 'Helpful Signs', 'The Poignant', 'Sandpiper' and 'Lost for Words'. All of the others are more obscure but at least hint at some aspect of the subsequent Ukrainian scenario. Those that fall into this latter category have been 'stolen' and adapted from other poems that I have written. Indeed, some of them relate to subjects far removed from Ukraine – subjects that provided me with a necessary diversion from the intensity of my focus on war. Whatever, I hope the introductory poems prepare you for the main event.

Throughout the six-week period, the habit of listening and writing became compulsive. It became a most draining process, as reflected in my musings on depression ('The Wire' and 'Swaying on the Wire') and the whole business of heartfelt tears ('The Poignant' and 'Butchers of Bucha'). At times, I could not write. The sentiments expressed in 'Stalemate', where neither progress in the outcome of war, nor its ending, was apparent, reflect the stalemate of my mindset at that time. I did not know which way to turn. I needed encouragement and found it.

The actual listening to events as broadcast had its own hardships, but these are, of course, a common feature of our current world and media access. I was not alone in experiencing the blow-by-blow horror of what was being reported. I found that writing an account (taking notes) on what I was hearing to be fairly straightforward. I hope that

I understood accurately the factual basis to my poems. These notes were immediately and quickly transcribed into a fairly dense prose poetry. Some of this seemed adequate to the task of conveying the raw sentiment of the moment and has remained largely untouched. An exception has been the introduction of line breaks (often following prepositions) that facilitated a stark (and essentially free-standing) statement in the next line. At times, the prose poetry seemed far too dense and more like a minute of war-reporting, without much 'edge' to enhance the message. Where I found this to be the case, I played with verse forms (mostly line lengths and rhythm) until I found something pleasing that enhanced the sentiment and flow of my writing. You will decide if and where I have succeeded or otherwise.

I have stopped writing (at least for just now) given that the 'first phase' appears to have been concluded. It is not my place to comment on strategies and outcomes, but it does seem as if the initial blitz on many fronts is now focussing on eastern Ukraine. The death toll is horrific, and the associated grief of survivors defies comprehension. Parts of the country are completely and utterly in ruins. Life is destroyed. And the bombardment continues. I see no end in sight for so long as Putin and his cronies remain in the Kremlin.

100% of royalties from this book will be donated directly to Hope and Homes for Children, an international charity working in Ukraine since 1998 to ensure each child can enjoy the safety and belonging of a loving family home, never an orphanage.

The Edge of Naivety

Primrose and Claw
Crying for Kharkiv

It is early spring and winter breathes its last. I am in the north of Scotland and hope to catch fish. But my trip to the north is much more than that. In fact, catching fish is only a very small part of my venture. This is a time of renewal, a time when I seek (and invariably find) renewed strength for the coming year. I bask in the total atmosphere of the place and find joy in the smallest hints of rebirth. I approach the river and climb up its valley before scrambling down to the Falls pool. Most years it will hold salmon. Every year on its sunny rock face it sports bright yellow primrose, beautiful tokens of seasonal awakening. It is also a place where the bobbing flight of grey wagtails (bright yellow in hue) can be invaded by the deadly flight of a focussed sparrowhawk. It does not miss its prey. So, my spring awakening is one of expectation, beauty, joy and death. Beauty and death going hand in hand.

I sense this is what the child in Kharkiv experienced in seeing the beauty of a bright star and assuming it to be yet another deadly missile. More cause for her ongoing distress. Likewise, the child, confused by the beauty of a flower by the perimeter of a prison fence: Stars and flowers, things of beauty to our eye, stars, as part of a wondrously self-ordered macro-universe, flowers, the manifestation of self-assembly at the microscopic scale. I would rather marvel at the complex beauty of galaxies and flowers than dwell on the crude string-pulling of the autocratic puppet-master that is Putin.

Primrose and Claw

At my cheek, hard pressed on rock,
bright-yellow primrose herald spring.
The warmth of radiating rock
allowing these joyful harbingers.
Rainbow spray before my eyes,
light show that makes the river sing.
Sobering touch of wing and claw.
Here sparrow hawk will nail its prey.
Stunning hit in narrow gorge
of wagtail on its morning flight.
Feathered yellow on dull-named grey,
that sullies primrose where it shines.

Crying for Kharkiv

The embarrassing comfort of
my radio armchair.
Heard a man from Kharkiv
experience the shuddering horror of
Russian shelling.
Thundering shakes, wailing sirens
had become this man's norm.
Flashing lights, dark night sky.
Two days of Putin, distorted memory.
Currency of war.
Told me his young daughter took fright
at yet another light.
A tiny twinkle in
the darkest extremity of high heaven.
Innocence ran scared.
Moved to tell her lovingly that
what she saw was a star.
A shining body far beyond
the mad reach of Putin's wildest dream.
Constancy in life.
Reminded me of a war child
looking through the hard wires of

her captivity.
Staring at the barren dir. of prison camp.
Somewhere on the edge.
Spying something small that shone bright and
free on the other side.
"What's that?" she asked surprised.
"It's a flower," came the compassionate reply.
Sign of ongoing life.
These two young girls do make me cry.
Tears shed for their honest,
youthful naivety.
Beauty of their ignorance in stars and flowers.
Things that do persist.
Thanks to the father from Kharkiv
who shared his broken heart.
Thanks to Leon Uris for
the single flower, a jewel found in the dirt.
Crying for Kharkiv.

The Bells of Hell

Saturation Point
Mariupol

In much of my day-to-day living, I pause and rest. I am tired in body and mind, so I have a break, perhaps fall asleep. I can take no more.

For those under siege in Mariupol, rest is not an option.

It's the horror of incessant war as it assaults the senses of those under attack. I know this to be true but cannot remotely imagine just how devastatingly bad it must be. These people have been plunged into a special sort of hell; a fate allotted to them by Putin as part of his freeing of a people. They do take more because their pride offers no option.

Saturation point

There comes a point when you
can take no more.
No more wine, women or song.
(And definitely no more tragedy.)
Incessant pressure
of raw circumstance.
Unyielding assault
on weak body and mind.
Enough heaven is enough heaven.
Enough hell is (already) too much hell.
And yet, it's not enough.
You do take more
because choice no longer reigns.
(Gone are the lazy days of summer ease.)
Your world is now a
pressure cooker hot.
The valve may leak but
the heat is always on.
You evaporate in clouds of steam
because you cannot purge the heat to boil.

Mariupol

Mariupol under siege.
The peace of life trashed overnight.
Four hundred thousand dance with fate,
Music not their choice.
Discretion not for age or sex.
Some fit (or so they used to be).
Dependents with their silvery wire.
Loud cries of fledgling babes.
Old and infirm try to move
in cold and dark that does not yield.
Broken bodies confronted by
one step now too far.
For some a merciful release,
their bodies slowly shutting down.
Those younger, angry with despair
at what they are denied.
Shelling of maternity,
assault on those that bring new life.
The pain of giving birth in war.
Wards a place of death.
The dice now thrown for one or both.
Young mother dies beside her child

or newborn babe assumes the cold.
Perhaps dice roll for both.
Bodies rotting in the street,
Some bloated under rubble graves.
Those bagged, dropped awkwardly in pits.
Any space will do.
Putin's special operation.
A liberation of deceit.
The stench of war without resource.
Starvation, thirst and cold.

Motherhood

Unexpected Rowan
A Putin Child

I am in the ancient woodlands of Glen Affric, Scotland. It is a truly most beautiful place that surprises by its rugged assemblage of rocks and plants. Here you find trees, mosses and lichens growing in the most incongruous of places. Pine thrives on bare bedrock with little evidence of soil. I find a large rowan growing on the branch of an equally mature birch. It is the most stunning and weirdest example of epiphytic living. Apparently, if you are a small seed-bearing fruit, you cannot always choose your site of procreation.

I suspect that the lady giving birth to her child in the bombed-out basement of some Putin-trashed building might smile wryly at the utter incongruity of her situation – the ad hoc nature of her maternity. Procreation on the wing. I hope she and her family have lived to smile.

Unexpected Rowan

The unexpected rowan, the sporadic rowan.
Growing on the rock.
Growing on dead trunk, growing on a living tree.
Perched incongruously
in snug cradling arms of birch.
Chance placement of fruit by passing jay.
Precarious installation of nature.
Birch carries rowan.
The lady bears an unexpected child.
Cream plates of summer flowers.
Brimming ripe-red autumn fruit.
Tangled serendipity of life.

A Putin Child

The lady has waited
seventeen long years.
She and her partner,
trying, praying, hoping for
a child.
And now
the miracle has happened.
She has become
a mother.
A birth,
not as she had planned (last week) in
the safe nest of
a maternity ward.
No, the woman has given birth to
her baby daughter in
some shelled-out basement.
(Perhaps this was the maternity ward.)
A bird dropping an egg in
flight.
The woman lies exhausted,
smiling the tearful smile of
a new mother.

She turns her dishevelled gaze lovingly to
the bedside cot.
The innocence of
a newborn daughter to
her touch.
The miracle child is
so vulnerable in
her maternal dependence.
But she is alive.
Her mind is exposed,
an open book.
Myriad pathways established in
response to
an environment of war.
The love of her mother attempting to
smother the explosions and rumbles,
the shrieking and screaming,
the wailing of
grief.
This is the infant's early life,
the formative years.
The years from which the love for
her mother will blossom.
Likewise, her hatred of
Putin.
Her mother and father are
considering names but
cannot agree.
Victoria (Victory) or Nadiya (Hope)

are being discussed.
Perhaps they will choose both.
I hope they are still relevant.

Death Masks

The Fear of Death
Walking the Plank

One thing I do know is that one day I shall die. I don't know when the axe will fall but I know it will happen. In the meanwhile, I keep going, living on the assumption that the present moment will not be my last. I tend not to dwell too much on this. I go on as before.

For the people of Ukraine, the issue is more urgent and persistent. To survive, they must move. For many, the flight is on foot – aching feet trudging on to who knows where. They are of all ages and degrees of infirmity. Some can barely walk but they do their best. I cannot imagine their pain, the physicality of it all cloaked in grief. They all walk the metaphorical plank of Putin's evil. For some, they must also walk the real plank of improvised timber across rushing torrents. They do not all survive.

The Fear of Death

We (mostly) do not search for death.
It finds us without our help.
We know that death will snare us all,
a case of how and when.
For some, a sudden unknown hit.
For some, the long-drawn exit.
The knowledge that all is not well.
A call to arms for self.
Singleness of stark nakedness,
Confronted by sure-fire death.
For some, the sudden fall of axe,
the practised blade on neck.
Others sweat, digging shallow grave.
Firing squad, proximal trench.
For them, the shot in back of head.
A fall in self-dug pit.

Walking the Plank

The need to move,
whatever the challenge.
Escape from
the shelling and the rubble.
No power, no water, no food.
Escape from the stench
of bodies
and fear of death.
But no escape from grief.
Grief goes with them.
Embodiment of grief.
Elderly,
infirm who can barely walk.
Excruciating pain in hips.
Stiff arthritic knees,
shooting ache
with every step.
Extreme sciatic stabs.
Ulcerating legs
that blister bleed in
agony of
unaccustomed standing.

Gone the solace of yesterday,
comfort of raised bed.
Sweet relief through
lying down with
elevated feet.
Catheter tubes,
bags not meant for walking.
Swaying with
little or no sure balance.
Somehow, they must put one foot in
front of the other.
Hard, cold boots that
blister feet.
Old feet, bleeding sores.
Survivors have
no choice in what remains.
Cold darkness of
night punctuated by
glimmers of daylight, incessant
freeze-thaw of winter.
Snow and puddles.
Water of life
slaking parched, cracked lips.
Moments of low
bright sun that's never warm.
Light that does
not heat but still blinds the eye.
Need a bridge, river to be crossed.
But there is no bridge.

Makeshift structure of
naked boards.
Torrents rush below.
Infirm must walk
this plank of piracy.
Putin's plank of
fervent will and motion
Minds aware, legs not responding,
bodies shake and fall.
Cradled safe in
transient arms,
angel wings bestow.
Others fall by
the bridge too far.
For some, the
stumbling walk of death goes on.
Assumption of something better,
The eternal hope.
One foot after
stuttering foot.
Way beyond the pain.
Encouragement.
Talk human corridors,
green passage.
Escape darkest Putin hell.
Where is the green beyond the bridge?
Shelling starts again.
There is no green.
Lie after lie.

Putin's brute deceit.
Nothing behind.
No future lies ahead.
Just the roar
and dreadful pain of war.
Another lie from the cesspit of
humanity,
To lie down now
would bring respite.
Best defy the beast.

A Sense of Belonging

*Plovers in the Spring
Sanity*

I am back in the north of Scotland. It is early springtime and I seek the assurance of renewal. I need to belong, to know that I matter. My assurance comes as the plovers return, running fast beside the stones as they claim their territory in the wind and sunshine. I do not know if I suffer from mental illness. Perhaps I do but it is not a source of great worry. I belong.

Others are less fortunate. The Tourette sufferer of whom I hear feels lost. His outbursts mean that he does not fit the norm. He does not belong. But now he is in the company of those who scream, those in Ukraine who run frightened by Putin's onslaught. The doctor comforts the man as he comforts others and in this they both retain their sanity. Now they both belong.

Plovers in the Spring

Searching for plovers in the stones.
I look for them and they find me.
Running low on sheep-cropped grass,
their voices beckoning afar.
An expectation now fulfilled.
Knowing that spring has found its step.

Sanity

A Ukrainian doctor in
the grip of war.
Surrounded by
the frightened, the distressed, the wounded,
the dead and the grieving.
He tells the reporter that
he must work to
avert the dull anger and grief that
surrounds him.
He must work to avert
despair.
His despair.
More people arriving
seeking shelter and aid.
Ever more people.
And into this throng comes a man whose
isolation and protection have been shattered.
A man who suffers from
Tourette syndrome.
A man whose
embarrassing convulsions and outbursts
were previously confined to

some home now destroyed.
The man has followed the throng for days.
Followed at a distance,
a sense of not belonging.
But now he is here in
the arms of the doctor
who knows him to be harmless.
Surrounded by
so many who now
shake and scream
as never before.
The man now belongs.
He should no longer feel
inadequate.
Our doctor finds sanity in
the care of the insane.
Otherwise, his life falls apart.

Beauty of the Absurd

The Incongruous
The Wedding Guest

I fish for grayling in the winter of Scottish rivers. The scene is magical with shining icicles and hard frozen ground. I need some indication of what's happening below the water's surface so I fish with a small bright red float. It seems so incongruous (by design) in its watery surrounds.

Orla arrives at the wedding of two young Ukrainians, those who wish to tie the knot in a time of war. How strange that seems; the incongruity of normality in the midst of chaos. Stranger still, a wedding with flowers and champagne amidst the rubble. A declaration of defiance. I congratulate the young couple (and Orla)!

The Incongruous

And then,
the incongruous.
The tiny, bright-red stem of
balsa float, flagging the progress of
bait below.
Long rod held high, vain hope of
keeping fine line dry.
Trotting the stream,
watching for red in
the hope that it might disappear.
Eyes straining in
low-arcing sun for
the distant offering,
the float no longer seen.

The Wedding Guest

The usual deafening noise of
shelling.
Sometimes distant, sometimes close.
It only took a few days for
this to become the new norm.
Putin's non-war on
Ukraine.
His liberation of a folk from
their freedom.
The travesty of
an empire builder.
The absurdity of
the deluded.
Enter our young bride and groom.
Both dressed in combat fatigues.
She wearing a white veil.
Red carnations and champagne bottles.
(How did they survive the shelling?)
The taking of vows, the singing,
the smiles and laughter amongst
friends.
A short interlude to test the reality of

a previous life.
And into this small gathering comes
Orla, our reporter of standing.
Never scared to take a stance,
often controversial. Orla whose
looks have not changed in twenty years.
Her haggard face that
has always shown concern,
an inscrutable beauty of her own.
"Orla Guerin, BBC," she says and
congratulates the newlyweds.
Orla has become a guest,
a witness to intention,
an instrument of enquiry.
The beautiful and urgent absurdity of
the moment is now complete.
The meeting of
past and present lives.
The commitment to
a future, whatever that might be.
Dali should have been here to capture
the surrealism of the moment.
Dali with his fine feel for
colour, perfect lines and perspective.
The flow of absurdity
that is our norm.
I shall leave them now.
Orla will go her own relentless way,
exploring and reporting on

further confrontation.
The young couple will engage in
war,
knowing that their love for
one another
has been declared.
What more can be said?
A moment past.
A moment that must be remembered.

Suffer the Little Children

Stained Glass Terror
Chemical Warfare

It is strange what I remember from my early childhood. I live in a large house. On the stair landing there is a stained-glass window with deep reds and blues shining on the carpet flooring. The box room is dark but, with eyes blinded by the stained-glass sun, green lights seem to flash in its darkness. The scare of darkness is enhanced by the turned face of a screaming girl on the page of some wayward magazine. I know that, if I rock my head on the pillow at night, the dim-orange bulb of the ceiling lamp will dance and its patterns will protect me from danger. I do not wish to be ill.

Others are less fortunate. They are already ill. They have no need of rocking heads and dancing oranges. They need medication or they will die. Such is the lot of hundreds of Ukrainian children, young lives who are dying because they cannot get medication as prescribed. Killing by denying access to chemicals. A new type of chemical warfare initiated by Putin. Does he care? I doubt it.

Stained Glass Terror

The stained-glass dance of red and blue.
Eyes tightly shut and pressed upon.
Dark cupboard space with flashing green,
a scare of goblins in the black.
Great staring eyes of screaming girl.
The death-bound door of fiction real.
A rocking head and dancing lamp.
A chain of orange to save myself.
Orange-chain ritual to deter what
surely lurked beneath my bed.

Chemical Warfare

Young children that are different.
Some emaciated in
treatment.
Eyes bulging and staring.
Others strangely bloated by
inflammatory response.
Most bald or with
scant patches of
hair yet to be shed.
All sufferers of
some cancer.
All undergoing treatment.
The distress and hope of
chemotherapy.
The distress and hope of
parents.
Therapy now stopped as
these young lives embrace
the westbound exodus.
The hard, cold slog of
mean evacuation.
The slow, weak trail of

nausea and sickness.
Resigned confusion of
the dependent.
The tears of
a young Polish doctor who
opens her arms to
these children.
She has been pushed to
her limits under
the increasing burden of numbers.
Trying to treat and prioritise with
the resources she has.
She knows that not all can be saved.
A new type of
chemical warfare.
Killing by deceit.
Killing by denial.
Killing of the young (not to mention the old) by
disruption to chemical supply.
A Putin strategy
that is adequate to
his inadequacy.

Reaching for the Sky

Surging Upwards
Needing Air

I find myself in Affric, strenuously walking upwards over hard rock hummocks and wetter moss hollows. The cover of heather is deep and springy and makes the going tough. I feel as if I am wading in a swelling sea that throws me to the floor. Above me is the tree canopy, a waving sea of birch and pine. Above that, the sky is bright.

The lady in Ukraine is confined to her dark basement, sent there by her Russian intruders. A prisoner in her own house. The incessant noise of shelling in the dark has become her life. And then it is quiet. Tentatively, she reaches for the stair and starts to climb. Soaring like a swimmer from the dark depths to the light above. The sky is bright.

Surging Upwards

Tentative steps into
the ancient woodland.
Winding stairways of
the imagination that
few have trod.
Surging upwards through
waist-deep swathes,
wading onwards in
Atlantic swell with
clawing arms and thighs.

Needing Air

The distant rumble becomes
an immediate roar and shaking.
The onslaught of
Putin's war.
Except it's not a war,
just an absurd denazification
(Putin jargon) in
Putin's dream.
The eternity of
war.
(Or was it just two days?)
How long will this last?
And then
Putin's soldiers come.
How old are they?
Do they know what they are doing?
Do they share in
Putin's dream?
Ordering the lady and her family to
the basement of
her house.
Soldiers occupying her world.

Bright heaven above,
dark hell below.
The shelling intensifies.
Thunderous roaring,
shattering and shaking
all around.
Some of it very close.
Some of it extremely close.
Deafening.
And then,
it becomes quieter,
an uncertain lull in
the storm.
Will it last?
The lady needs air.
She is coming up for
air.
Needing to gulp
that raw freshness like
a diver from
the depths.
Stumbling from
the cold darkness below, to
a heaven of
light and air.
If only she could swim, clinging to
the diver in
ascent.
It is suddenly so bright.

The lady blinded by
the intensity of
light.
Bewildered as her eyes adjust,
astonished by
the switch from
hell to heaven.
She is looking at
the sky.
The cold, blue sky of
a late winter's morning.
There is no roof to
her house.
No roof to
heaven.
Heaven now
a brighter version of
hell.
There is plenty of air for
the lady.
Everything destroyed.
Her living space,
her furniture,
her belongings,
pictures of
family continuity.
Her life.
All trashed.
The only thing enhanced is her hatred of

Putin.
Is this what he means by
denazification?

The Act of Living

Composure
Lunch in Kharkiv

I often find it difficult to say what I really mean. I am too spontaneous in my response to questions of health and well-being. Always replying positively when I should be expressing doubt or offering a truer picture of my innermost feelings. Perhaps I am protecting those who ask from the confusion of my mind. I portray a picture of composure from within my chaotic self.

The young lawyers in Kharkiv are confronted by this dilemma as their apartment is trashed by Putin. I understand why the lady responds so positively to her daughter's casual enquiry. I would (unthinkingly) have done the same. It is how she is. It is how I am.

Composure

Sometimes it is better that
we do not share reality.
Share what really is so awful.
Do not share the darkness.
Hard circumstance and illness become
our bubbles of
discretion.
Ways of
hiding, running from
the truth.
Small capsules of
survival.
Is this a good thing?
We do not dwell on
sudden hardship or devastation.
"How are you doing?"
"Fine. Yourself?"
The glorious salvation of
spontaneity.
(Didn't give that any thought at all.)
What we really mean,
we cannot express.

The utter devastation that we feel.
The depths we cannot share.
Consternation of
reality.
Hidden life within
the bubble we call self.
Life (sort of) goes on.
Death is (very much) in
the offing.
I desperately need another bubble.
A prescription for
composure.

Lunch in Kharkiv

Two young lawyers, in
their Kharkiv-centre apartment.
Drawing chairs to
the table, set for
lunch.
Bottle of
red
providing a modicum of
normality.
The familiarity of
explosions confined to
the distance, round
the perimeter of
their city.
The new normality for
our lawyers.
Was the sun shining?
What did they talk about?
What were they thinking?
The weather?
Their family?
Their health?

I assume their focus was on
Putin's non-war and its pressing implications.
But life sort of
goes on for
our professional couple.
They feel a measure of
safety until
the hit comes.
The sudden blinding flash and roar.
The incredible shaking of
building and body.
The balcony ripped from
its frontage.
Glass flying, bodies thrown.
Blood everywhere.
The collapse of
furniture and fixtures.
Dust everywhere.
Their refrigerator playing tunes as it rolls down
the corridor.
Instant mayhem.
They scramble from
their apartment onto
the street.
Pulling bits of
glass from
their cuts.
The woman's phone rings.
It is her daughter, phoning from

a sport's camp.
"Everything okay, Mum?"
The mother pauses.
"Yes, darling, everything's fine."
Putin may destroy their infrastructure.
He may displace millions.
He may injure and kill but, for
so long as one Ukrainian lives,
he will not break the spirit of
this nation.

Dignity

*Lady of the Trees
Svetlana's China*

I love the slender, shifting beauty of birch in all its seasons.
It is a tree with poise, a tree of dignity.

I see Svetlana in her high-rise apartment as I see birch.
Svetlana is a lady of dignity. Her house has been shelled
by mad Putin but her precarious furniture, a dresser with
its fine display of porcelain, survives. She has been hurt by
Putin but she holds him in disdain. She has soared above
anything he might do to her. A lady of beauty and dignity.
Like birch, Svetlana is a class act in all seasons.

Lady of the Trees

The stunning contrast of
birch and pine.
Birch, the lady of
our trees.
Her white limbs
mottled black and silver, with tresses of
twig and leaf washing in
the wind.
Her slender evening dress.
Glimpsing silver and yellow on
the sun-caught edges of
her slender frame.
Fresh green in
vibrant spring.
Worn green of
summer heat.
Bright yellow in
autumnal fall.
The subtle shades of
purple on
her winter nakedness.

Svetlana's China

Ten floors up in smouldering Kharkiv.
Soaring above the gruesome
rubble dust of Putin.
A fragile nest
high in the city canopy.
Here sways Svetlana.
Now in her seventies.
Svetlana surveys her apartment.
A bird securing her perch.
On one side, windows smashed,
the room destroyed.
She must seek refuge and scant sleep
in her other room.
Remarkably intact.
It's here we find Svetlana's china.
Most incongruent display,
fine porcelain intact.
Fragility.
Cradled gently in the arms of
a magnificent dresser
(now bomb shelter).
Its very survival of bomb blast

declaring strong defiance.
A proclamation that
life's finer things
soar high above absurdity.
Horror of mad Putin.
Fine things really matter.
She has nothing to say to Putin.
Svetlana has no words for
the evil of Putin.
Dismissed him as
filth, not worthy of her comment.
Cries of gratitude,
soldiers to her defence.
Soldiers numbering her two daughters
and her young granddaughter brave.
Ordinary folk who
have risen to
the challenge, national defence.
How many Svetlanas?
Swaying but still intact.
Those who still survive in Kharkiv hell,
Mariupol and elsewhere in
this fine-cultured land.
Intact dresser.
Fine china survives bombardment.
Cameo defiance,
Dignity with beauty.

The Place of Death

The Corner Pool
Twice a Hostage

I walk the winter river bank and disturb a salmon kelt, a fish that has spawned but is not yet dead. It may survive and return to the oceans where it will feed and regain strength. This is indeed possible but unlikely to be the case. It is more likely that the fish will die in the effort. A fish in the departure lounge of its travels. I wish its life might slip away without undue stress.

I hear of an elderly Ukrainian lady, lying bedridden in what remains of her shelled apartment. She is utterly dependent on the help of her loving daughter. The lady survived Hitler in the siege of Leningrad. First Hitler, now Putin. I think it might be better if she slept the eternal sleep but the lady hangs on in her defiance of Putin.

The Corner Pool

The corner pool,
steep-sloped with shaded edge.
Skirting the ice,
Old kelt disturbed,
The tattered fins of
last year's run.
It's always there,
just hanging on to life.
A long swim from
the distant sea
it may never find.
Better dead.

Twice a Hostage

A veteran of Leningrad from the nineteen forties.

The siege of Leningrad.

Extreme minimal rations of occasional food, mostly inedible.

Starvation, pain and death.

Never forgotten but all now revisited.

A young girl who should be blossoming in her early adolescence.

But Hitler thought otherwise.

She survived more than two years of siege.

The destruction of her city.

The destruction of her people.

The destruction of her youth.

She is now in her nineties.

(What happened in the intervening years?)

An old woman with her early memories.

Unable to move from her Ukrainian apartment.

Again, under bombardment.

The exhaustion of shelling.

The cold, the dark, now past hunger.

This time, at the mercy of Putin.

She lies in her bed, propped pink against a spartan wall.

She cannot move.

Did pictures once hang here?

Was there once a vase of flowers?

Her daughter tends (as best she can) her mother's needs.

Slight movement to salve the sores.

Gentle bathing when water allows.

Whatever nourishment she can find.

The orchestra of falling shells.

The stuttering andante of failing life.

A touching of hands.

The daughter leaves but will return.

At least that is her intention.

To do that, she must be alive.

And that is not certain.

The only certainty is that things are getting worse,

as they once did for her mother in Leningrad.

The daughter cannot say this, but I shall.

If only the old lady's frail body would dream its final
dream,

she might be spared this horror.

The travesty of reliving her childhood

in the cold darkness of despair.

A hostage to further siege.

For her, death can only bring relief.

But she is not dead.

Not yet.

In living weakly,

she waves the flag of strong defiance in Putin's storm.

The Inappropriate

Convenience of Conscience
Ministries of Embarrassment

I live in a world of convenience, a world of contrived social structures, what I call society. It is a world of hierarchy, rules and regulations. A world of apparent (or not so apparent) convenience. A world that can, perhaps inadvertently, block the implementation of what I think is humane. In the realm of bigger society, my conscience can die.

I listen with embarrassment to the bureaucratic nonsense associated with refugee entry from Ukraine to the U.K. The stance of our Home Office seems so inadequate in face of the immediate crisis of the displaced. We should not forget that this is our Home Office, part of our elected Government. Perhaps slowly, the whole cumbersome hierarchy with all its machinations is aligning itself with the voice of those individuals who care. A response to conscience. I can only hope so.

Convenience of Conscience

Contrary to common perception,
most of our organisations –
our apparent aggregations and hierarchies of mind –
are all myths of the Harari kind.
Figments of our imagination,
conveniences of conscience,
cloaks of selfish deceit
that aim to categorise for some purpose.
A purpose that is rarely transparent.

Ministries of Embarrassment

The red tape of officialdom can be so embarrassing.
So inappropriate to the crisis.
Witness the U.K. response to
the immediate needs of Ukrainian refugees.
Three weeks of Putin's non-war and
three million women, children and the elderly
have fled their country.
Three million people in distress.
Three million bewildered citizens of
a resolute Ukraine.
Our European neighbours have done well.
Welcoming of refugees with
open arms and hospitality.
Securing entry.
Paperwork to be dealt with at a later date.
Poland has been a shining example.
Food, shelter and warmth for the stranger,
the starving, the cold and the distraught.
The U.K. has insisted on a visa process with
its associated plethora of form filling and verification.
Our Home Secretary has insisted on
a strict vetting of entrants.

A bureaucratic kick in the teeth for
a homeless neighbour.
Surely not all infants and the elderly are
would-be terrorists?
We did do something.
Not immediately but in response to modest demand.
We set up visa centres such as the one in Calais.
(At least, so we were told.)
A place to which the war-shocked citizen
might come and seek refuge in the U.K.
In practice, a place to which scant few arrived.
The redirecting to Brussels with
a bag of crisps and a chocolate biscuit.
(Opening times Wednesday, Thursday, Friday.)
Public stirrings in the U.K.
Voices of dissension.
Utter disbelief at
the inadequacy of Westminster response.
The ongoing contrast between
the U.K. response and that of
European neighbours.
An embarrassing comparison.
Enter our Minister for Transport.
Why?
(Sure, there might be an issue of
transportation into the U.K.)
Our Minister tells us that
President Zelensky wishes refugees to
remain close to Ukraine.

Fine.

Except it's not fine.

Are we using this as some weak coat-hanger of
an excuse to admit fewer refugees?

Fewer of those who will die if
they do not receive aid.

One extra hour of air flight back to Ukraine at
some future date.

Does this one hour really matter?

Or do we expect our refugees to
walk back to their homeland?

This argument appears to have gone quiet amidst
further stirrings of popular discontent.

And now we have a Minister for Refugees.

(Is this an admission that our other offices were
     inadequate?)

I wish him well.

An immediate call for intimations of
volunteers to house refugees in the U.K.

Within one day, we have more than
one hundred thousand offers of accommodation.

A reflection of the true compassion of our country for
their neighbours in need.

A proper response despite
the embarrassment of earlier ministerial claims.

Playing Safe

Helpful Signs
Visit to the Theatre

I live in a world of signs, a world of commands, warnings, adverts of danger or joy. I am the product of an evolutionary process where the response to signals is important to my survival. Otherwise, I would not be here. However, like all others, I have a free will. I can ignore the signals. I do not have to obey, even if the signs are meant to be helpful.

I hear that families are seeking refuge in the theatre of Mariupol, refuge from the incessant onslaught from the sky. Clear signage on the ground, to be seen from the sky, declares the presence of children in the theatre building. Putin chooses to ignore this. He kills as he pleases in the pursuit of his aims (whatever those really are).

Helpful Signs

Our world is littered with information,
supposedly helpful.
"Danger, overhead wires!"
"Dangerous currents, no swimming!"
"Beware, rabies!"
"Beware of the bull!"
And so on.
Mostly, we pay heed to such signs and
behave accordingly.
But sometimes we ignore them, for
whatever reason.
Careless inattention or wilful disregard.
Sometimes the consequences are
dire.

Visit to the Theatre

A safe place to shelter when
you have nowhere else to hide.
The white splendour of Mariupol's theatre.
The former place of fantasy, hope and inspiration.
Now a place for women and children to
escape the incessant destruction of
their city.
A basement safe from
Putin's pounding.
Except it is not safe.
A well-flagged refuge for
the weak and innocent.
A place of sanctuary for
young children who do not understand this war.
(Putin's special operation, his non-war.)
And from the sky, clear signage on
the ground declaring children,
children at the building's edge.
What does the aggressor not understand?
A statement clear
A massive hit.
Total destruction.

Demolition.
Don't think of the building.
Think of the one thousand
who took refuge there.
The tragedy of one thousand.
Many still buried in the rubble.
Perhaps three hundred dead.
Perhaps more.
We must assume instant death for some,
slow painful death for others.
Very slow and very painful.
So many more injured.
Did anyone escape death?
There is not much left of Mariupol.
Many have now fled
what once was home.
But many remain in
the utter devastation of their city.
The mercy missions find access blocked by
Putin's rats.
In consolidating his gains in the East,
will Putin suffocate the last breaths of
the one hundred thousand who remain in
Mariupol?
Does he care?

Displacement

Hard Edge to Beauty
Exodus to Lviv

I am back in Affric, one of my favourite places. Its lichens string beauty in the branches of its bows as pine and birch sway in unison in the summer wind. But even in this most beautiful of places, suffering and death are not that far away. As I walk in the woodland, I find the remains of a deer. Its death cannot have been peaceful.

I see pictures of the mass exodus from eastern Ukraine to Lviv. People escaping the destruction of Putin while still alive. Mostly women, children and the elderly moving as best they can. Nobody can find it easy leaving everything they possess but for some the hardship is extreme. None more so than those who already carry the scars of Putin's war.

Hard Edge to Beauty

There is a hard edge to this beauty.
A tempering of its appeal.
Sheer moss-clad faces dropping into the pit.
Thin layers of fallen twigs and leaves
littering the treacherous surface.
Uncertain webs of decay
hiding clefts between the rocks.
Trapdoors underfoot for the unwary.
The remains of last year's fallen stag,
bones scattered where it fell.
Its broken shin still
caught between two rocks.
A horrendous death through
pain, starvation and thirst.
The ravages of winter storm.
The destruction that is part of
who we are.

Exodus to Lviv

The train is packed.
A track full of refugees from the East
carrying their meagre possessions.
Normal people who had been getting on with
the ups and downs of life.
Normal people until Putin came.
Now they have nothing.
Well, nearly nothing.
What do you take?
A wash bag, a tooth brush?
(Will there be water?)
Some underwear and socks?
Extra shirt, jersey and trousers?
Spare boots?
Spare hat and gloves to
thwart the freezing cold?
What about some keepsakes?
Family photographs, small valuables?
(Things that make you who you are.)
Is there room for all of this?
Don't forget your phone.
(Can it be charged?)

Some money and a passport
(if you have one).
Oh, and don't forget
you'll be carrying a huge bundle of
grief (your heaviest item).
You are one of two hundred thousand
seeking shelter in Lviv to the West.
Perhaps you met the
eighty-six-year-old grandmother,
small and frail, leaning on her stick,
leaning on her loving granddaughter.
She carries massive bruising to her face
having tripped in a bomb shelter.
She has left behind Mariupol and
its total destruction.
Dead bodies on the street and under rubble.
Buildings smashed,
roads destroyed and
trees uprooted.
Or perhaps you noticed the younger lady,
the amputee with her children.
She lost her leg during
Putin's adventures in
twenty fifteen.
This is the second time
she has been made homeless.
The second time she has been
on the run (as best she can).
Those who arrive in Lviv can marvel at

its bizarre installation of strollers
arranged poignantly in a city square.
One stroller for each infant killed.
These are the documented dead.
The number of dead toddlers
that increases by the day
How do these ordinary folk view Putin?
The autocrat who is carrying out a
denazification of their land.
The man who is saving them from
their folly of free will.
The man who is restoring them to
their rightful place in
his declared common spiritual space of
Russia, Belarus and Ukraine.
He should front up and try telling that to the face of
the two hundred thousand, the granny with
her smashed face and the lady amputee.

Play Acting

Harari Myths
Putin Rally

I love the writings of Yuval Noah Harari. In recent years he has brought a refreshing lucidity to my understanding of human behaviour and the organisations we create. For most of our evolution, we have not lived in large, organised societies. These are fabrications (Harari myths) for which, in a biological or psychological sense, we are not adapted. Small wonder we make a mess of things! How can it be that people (in their thousands) hang on to the very words of autocrats who have climbed to the top of the pile? Surely, their myths (and those who believe them) are a manifestation of inadequacy and insanity in the human race – a species that is truly out of control.

Putin has become a master of deceit. He is also a master of manipulation. He knows how to play a crowd, how to disseminate lies and half-truths. He dreams a dream and shares it with millions. It is all that they hear, all that they know. Another glorious (or perhaps inglorious) myth is born. It may persist and cause unimaginable harm. Such has happened

Harari Myths

Government, society, religion,
systems of politics and economy.
All of these are Harari myths,
a consensus of contrived systems.
A consensus by
which we interact in
stumbling fashion, like drunks on
a homeward trail in
the blindness of
night.

Putin Rally

So, here we have it.
The Putin version.
The special operation.
The necessary and popular –
for those who believe him –
restoring of Ukraine to
its proper place.
The one shared spiritual space of
Russia, Belarus and Ukraine.
Russia's greatness under siege.
Putin the aggrieved.
Putin the saviour.
Putin the Great.
Echoes of the Kremlin newsfeeds.
"We do not bomb cities.
We do not kill children."
Try telling that to
the citizens of Ukraine.
And try telling that to
the thousands of Russians
who one day will hear of
their dead soldier son.

The little man struts on
stage as autocrats do.
(Think Hitler.)
Master of the moment.
Dictator of deceit.
Diverting blame for
any future hardship in Russia.
Not his fault.
Blame the decadent West.
Blame individual liberalism.
Blame NATO.
Punish dissident voices.
Suppress the media.
Disseminate untruths.
Deny rumours of aggression.
Promote ideas of 'them' and 'us',
traitors and patriots.
Lap up the milk of
ignorant adulation.
And while this parody of
a man plays to his public,
the non-war goes on.
The pounding and screaming that
cannot be heard in Moscow.
The death and suffering of
Ukrainians and Russians alike.
All the while digging the pit into which
he will fall or be thrown.
How can this man sleep?

Standing Still

Two-pronged Roar
Stalemate

I am back in the north of Scotland by a river that feels like home. Everything seems to be standing still, like the standing wave of a waterfall. I know the water is rushing through the pool but the fall itself seems static. I have a sense of unease.

It is the same with Ukraine and the reporting of its ongoing conflict. I know it's happening but it seems to be getting nowhere and I no longer feel the outrage. Have I become normalised and immune to the emotions of brutality? I hope not but I do not know. I have a creeping sense of stalemate with regard to the atrocities in Ukraine and the workings of my mind.

Two-pronged Roar

Down at the Falls,
the narrow ledge.
The rumble now
a two-pronged roar.
Rough edges to
the standing wave.
Fast water crashing
to the floor,
then pushing to
the shadow face,
before the quieter
glide at tail.

Stalemate

The uncertain time.
For four weeks,
my thoughts have been assaulted by
moments of poignancy.
Glimpses of Ukraine that
have made me cry.
Glimpses of Ukraine that
have filled me with anger.
But now, I feel much less.
Sometimes nothing.
Can I no longer feel the brutality of Putin?
Perhaps so.
Nothing seems to make me cry anymore.
Moments of poignancy have not found me.
I seem to have entered some steady state of
emotion where atrocities race through my mind without
affecting my overall state of
numbness.
Nothing seems to lift me to
a higher level or (perhaps mercifully) to
a lower place.
Perhaps I have already hit

emotional rock bottom.
I seem to be wading through treacle,
a slow, cumbersome effort
that takes me nowhere.
It's like looking at
a waterfall with standing waves.
Water thundering through
the abyss, but the shape of
the fall remains intact.
I sense this is what's happening in Ukraine.
Putin continues to pound the cities
but he makes no progress in
his overall aim (whatever that might be).
A gain here, a loss there.
The only things to increase being collaterals of
devastation to fabric and grief.
And my insensitivity.
So, we have arrived at
some stalemate of
progress and emotional state.
All thanks to the unshakeable will of
the Ukrainian people and
those who strive to help.
I doubt this steady state will last.
What will happen next?
Will the battle lines
be pushed back or broken?
Shall I remain in emotional limbo?
Shall I ever cry again?

The Edge of the Pit

The Wire
Swaying on the Wire

The pit begins to yawn showing the depths of its gullet and I am balancing on its wire. A sense of the proximity and imminence of the shadowlands pervades everything. I know this place and it is not a happy one. Such is my emotional state.

If dwelling on war is causing me depression, what must it be doing to the people of Ukraine? I feel desperate but I have friends who help restore in me a measure of sanity and hope. This is a depressive interlude but in the dark I now find glimmers of light and hope. It is not easy but I shall continue my quest, exploring the atrocity that is the onslaught of Putin on the Ukrainian people. Perhaps I shall dance again. Perhaps too, the people of Ukraine.

The Wire

Sometimes the dreary seems to
overwhelm all else.
There is no apparent spark of
joy or high excitement, but rather,
the all-encompassing mist of
the mundane pervades everything,
shunning the rich palette of
vibrancy that does not belong to
the shadowlands.
One treads with care at such times,
feet searching for
the wire, and arms widespread in
search of balance.
Always hoping to avoid
the pit of depression.
A whispering by the executioner in
his deceitful cloak.
A cloak that often seems a valid choice,
unless one has already tasted the dead space of
this dark void.
One day, the sun may shine again.
Perhaps, one day it will,

if one could only find the wire
somewhere between
the heights of exuberance and
the depths of despair.
Thanks to Kay Redfield Jamison.
Thanks to Karen.

Swaying on the Wire

Today, I know I'm losing balance.
Difficulty in walking the swaying wire.
The executioner welcoming me to the pit.
Calling me to end all of this.
Exhaustion, confusion,
sadness and so much more.
A sense of utter uselessness.
No fresh rain.
The rivers all run dry.
The need to stop.
In my isolation,
my broken heart cried.
I didn't know if you would hear.
I tried to find another way,
some weak romance.
You sent your heart.
It means the world to me.
A feeble sense of belonging.
An encouragement to persevere.
The need to flag humanity in
the tortured soul of Ukraine.
I shall continue.

I shall persevere in
pursuit of truth.
Ways of expressing the poignancy of
what is now reality.
Shining light on
the darkness of war.
I cry for Kharkiv.
I see Orla at the wedding.
I cross the river with the infirm.
I marvel at Svetlana's china.
The lady and I are coming up for air.
I can breathe again.
And I can cry.

The Well of Tears

The Poignant
Butchers of Bucha

Sometimes, I am shaken out of my complacency. Something gets through to me and I'm hurt. Something that knocks the mundane and makes me cry with anguish and anger – the poignant.

Iryna appears on my screen. She makes me cry in anger. A mother who has lost everything. Iryna is poignancy personified.

The Poignant

You might live in a palace with
all its trappings of luxury and comfort.
Sumptuous food and drink from
platters and goblets of silver.
Bizarrely, the luxurious becomes the mundane.
Or you might live in a cold, damp hovel
Where subsistence is the norm.
And you become used to it.
You live within a numb shell.
But occasionally, you are confronted by
something beyond
your accustomed realm.
Something that wakes you from
your complacency.
When this something makes you cry,
you have encountered the poignant.

Butchers of Bucha

Apparently, we're nearing the end of
the 'first phase'.
Russian troops appear to be departing from
their onslaught in
the neighbourhood of Kyiv.
A remarkable victory for Ukraine.
Referred to as
defeat of Russia (by Ukrainians) or
retreat of Russia (by Russians).
All of this matters not one iota for
Iryna who has lost her son.
Lost everything in Bucha.
Her son Oleksii was shot weeks ago as
he walked the five hundred metres between
house and work.
A lad of twenty-seven years who worked as
a tyre fitter.
Shot dead because he dared to walk.
Dared to earn a living.
Dared to support his mother.
Iryna fled because she had to.
Russian soldiers took over her house and

drank themselves silly on vodka and whisky.
Bottles thrown to the ground.
They have now gone and Iryna has returned.
A shell has destroyed Oleksii's room.
Iryna is all alone.
She has collected her dead Oleksii in
a wheelbarrow.
Wheeled him from the cold,
so that the dogs could
no longer get his body.
She has buried Oleksii in
a shallow grave in
her garden.
A grave that she dug herself.
A rug is placed over
the earthen mound.
It is topped with
a wooden palette, in
the hope that Oleksii's body will be safe.
Iryna is only forty-seven.
She looks at least twenty years older.
Her hands and nails are filthy from
war and burial.
She is clutching photos of
Oleksii to her breast.
Her love, her sweetheart, her provider.
Putin has left her nothing.
Absolutely nothing.
She wants Russians dead.

Wants their children to lie in the
dirt like her son.
We must leave Iryna
broken-hearted and devastated in
her grief. Crying loudly in
the swirling snow of
her chaotic life.
Standing in complete isolation.
She may not know it, but
there are hundreds like her.
People mourning in the wake of
the defeated butchers of Bucha.
Dead bodies lying,
bound and shot, food for
the vermin.
A scene of death for some.
For others, an
eternity of rape and torture.
I have learnt once more to cry in
grief and anger.

Complications of Simplicity

Grand Delusions
Defiance

I have learnt the lessons of grand delusion, the smoke and mirrors of our complicated lives. If only life were simpler, I would not need to lie. I wish I could tell the truth but life is complex (it has been since its very origins) and, very often, it is unnecessarily complicated and incomprehensible. We have made it so in recent phases of our evolution. A waving of hands because we cannot grasp reality. We cannot keep up with what we have created.

The lady seeking shelter in her bunker does not appear to be asking for much. Just give her space so that she can be self-sufficient. Her defiance goes beyond her hatred of Putin. She is making demands of simplicity that cannot be met in our complicated world. I wish it was otherwise.

Grand Delusions

Here, we can practise the grand delusions.
Creating the smoke and mirrors that
attempt to hide our gross inadequacy.
The failings of our behaviour in
defiance of our status.
Illusions of grandeur.
Castles in the sky.
Illusions that deflect from
the underlying truth that
we cannot grasp and
cannot manage the big picture in which
our boundless invention
outstrips our capacity to belong.
An oblivious but relentless pursuit of
self-destruction.

Defiance

The lady breeds rabbits for food.
She grows potatoes and vegetables.
She is self-sufficient.
She is surrounded by Putin's pounding.
Devastation all around her.
But she is not for moving.
She will not move for
that bully Putin.
She would rather die where she lives.
That may very well happen, now that
Putin's tide is turning east.
She cannot sleep in her house.
She deems that too dangerous.
So she sleeps deep in
a tiny brick bunker, her food store.
Here she can lie on sacks of potatoes,
surrounded by jars of pickled vegetables.
Not particularly comfortable,
not warm but relatively safe.
She is surrounded by
a plethora of religious icons and
prays for deliverance.

I cannot criticise her faith.
It is what keeps her going in
her defiance of the evil one.
That and rabbits,
potatoes and vegetables.
Here, we have a glimpse of
Europe in the twenty-first century.
The lady does not need a smart house,
smart car, smart phone or
smart anything.
She just needs a bit of
peace and quiet, and a space for
her animals and plants.
These commodities are in
short supply across Europe.
What little she asks for
may be far too much.

Failure of Humanity

Sandpiper
Kramatorsk Station

'Sandpiper' is one of my favourite poems of those that I have written. I think it sort of sums up who I am – mostly a well-intentioned idealist who normally fails. I think I'd rather be that than a conformist who never faces the dilemma.

Ukrainians on the run to Kramatorsk, fleeing with the hope of safe evacuation. Then the hit on the station killing hundreds, horrendous wounding of many more. The missile flagging 'For the Children'. Was this revenge or pure depravity? Perhaps it doesn't matter which it was. Whatever, it was yet another failure of humanity.

Sandpiper

I once stumbled upon a
sandpiper's nest.
Small cup with four eggs beside
the rising river.
I had not seen it before,
although I had
walked so close, so many times.
Blind to what I saw.
Now water lapped its edges.
My conscience stirred.
Eggs now moved to safer ground.
What else could I do?
Parent birds did not return.
The eggs turned cold.
Failure of humanity.
Is it always so?

Kramatorsk Station

Urged to flee.
Civilians on the run.
Some heeding this warning and
heading west while they can.
Grabbing bags,
as much as they can manage.
Older folks, women and children
fleeing the imminence of Putin.
Desperate to avoid the horrors of
Russian atrocity.
Four thousand people huddled in
the confines and surrounds of
Kramatorsk Station.
And then the hit.
The missile (or was it more than one).
The suspicion of cluster bombing,
the outlawed.
The explosions and fire.
At least fifty killed, including children.
Hundreds with horrendous injury to
head and stomach.
Legs and arms blown off.

The race to save lives.
The missile case with the painted words
'For the children'.
What on Earth does this mean?
In the ambiguity of war,
this is a new low.
A hit below the belt, even by
the nasty standards of Putin.
A confirmation of evil.
Where is safety now?

End of the Prelude

Lost for Words
Goodwill Gestures

I often find it difficult to choose words that express my deepest feelings. Perhaps I am too intent on crafting a phrase or sentence to capture some nuance. Sometimes it might be better if I just stated things as they are without any artistic clothing – the pure unadulterated horror of events.

It does seem as if there is a shift in Putin's placement of his troops. His legacy in the towns he is leaving is not pretty. See it as it is. The horror is raw, red blood and grief. He is upping his credentials as a war criminal supreme. I fear for the future.

Lost for Words

Moments in life (and death)
cannot always be expressed.
Words may prove inadequate.
We lack the tools to convey nuance,
capture the moment.
Music and art can help.
Poetry can expose the thread.
Sometimes it is best to let
stark statements release our emotions.
Let the heartache flow.

Goodwill Gestures

The war is moving east
The Donbas region.
It's more a case of continuing with
renewed vigour in the East.
Massive reinforcement,
regrouping of Russian forces.
Leaving Kyiv and other areas in the West.
A declaration of goodwill.
Apart from the looting,
raping and killing that
they leave in their wake.
The lady is worried sick for
her mother further up the street.
She is allowed to pass a blockade and
reaches her mother's house.
She tells the soldiers
she's been allowed to visit.
Her compassion is rewarded by
repeated shots to
her legs and genitals.
She is left for dead but survives.
One more atrocity.

Rape.
A weapon of war as always.
Women and girls.
Raped repeatedly in
the ruins of their life.
Raped in front of family.
Some huddled in captivity,
taken out repeatedly for rape.
Some now pregnant.
Disease.
The spoils of war.
The women have their own service of
remembrance.
The fucking rats move east.
Putin's boys.
Bodies crying under
piles of rubble in Borodyanka.
Friends and neighbours
not allowed near them.
Soon to be silent in their agony.
Perhaps not soon enough.
So many infants killed.
A grieving father.
A little two-year-old boy.
Past photos of him with his mother, as
she held his hands in
the summer sun.
A previous world.
He already knew his alphabet and

could count to ten.
His mother helping him walk beside
the summer flowers.
His last request was for
new sheets, the ones with stars.
Hopefully, his death was instant,
wrapped in his sheet of stars.
His sheet of death.
Close your eyes Orla,
lest you drown in tears.
The goodwill is focusing on the East.